OF THE
LOST & FOUND

*10 Reflections on Becoming
a Prayerful Human Being*

Aryeh Ben David

Other books by Aryeh Ben David

*Becoming a Soulful Educator: How to Bring Jewish
Learning from Our Minds, to Our Hearts, to Our
Souls—and Into Our Lives*

*Hearing Your Own Voice: The Ayeka Haggadah—
A Guide for All Ages to Personalize Your Seder*

*The Ayeka Shabbat: Hearing Your Own Voice—
A Guide for Personalizing Your Shabbat*

*Around the Shabbat Table: A Guide to Fulfilling and
Meaningful Shabbat Table Conversations*

The Godfile: 10 Approaches to Personalizing Prayer

Sasha,
Hope this helps you on
your spiritual journey!

PRAYERS
OF THE
LOST & FOUND

*10 Reflections on Becoming
a Prayerful Human Being*

Aryeh Ben David

אֵיכָה *Ayeka*

Prayers of the Lost & Found:
10 Reflections on Becoming a Prayerful Human Being

2019 Quality Paperback Edition, First Printing
© 2019 by Aryeh Ben David

ISBN: 978-0-578-53524-1

Design: Jen Klor, Jerusalem | jenklor.com
Cover and illustrations: Daphna Awadish | www.daphna-awadish.com

israel@ayeka.org.il | ayeka.org.il

Ayeka LTD
c/o Michal Smart
26 Toilsome Brook Rd.
Stamford, CT 06905-3952

I had a teacher in high school who asked me to write a poem.

She changed my life.

I don't remember her name.

This book is dedicated to her, wherever her soul may be.

In memory of Betty Meyers
Your laughter, spark, and generosity
continue to bring joy into our lives

CONTENTS

I

THE GOALS OF THIS BOOK

The goal of this book is not to help us "pray better," with greater intentionality or focus, but rather to help us become *prayerful human beings.*

This book addresses two pressing issues facing the Jewish world:

- The shrinking of our prayer life
- The absence of personal heartfelt conversations about our prayer life

The Shrinking of Our Prayer Life

We know how to pray the words. We know how to lead the services. But prayer is much more than the prayer book and synagogue services. We need to become prayerful human beings.

A prayerful person listens to God.

A prayerful person talks personally to God.

A prayerful person journeys.

A prayerful person is a work in progress.

A prayerful person is always becoming.

Once, a Jew prayed wherever, whenever, and however he or she wanted to pray. Prayer was a personal activity, an expression of one's condition, a full blending of one's inner and outer life. Words poured out, unplanned and unscripted; tears poured out, unafraid and uninhibited. Prayers emerged from the authentic human need to connect and converse with God. The act of prayer was not publicly regulated, nor did it come with societal pressures or expectations. There was no public norm. For over a thousand years the Jewish people prayed wherever, whenever, and however.

Then a radical disruption altered our prayer life. With Jerusalem destroyed and the Jewish people exiled from Israel, the rabbis felt compelled to "organize" prayer. This shared tradition would ensure the spiritual unity of the Jewish people during difficult times. Prayer, the natural and organic expression of our souls and relationship with God, became structured and systematized. The system included instituting a uniform synagogue blueprint, organizing a standard prayer service, and drafting the prayer book, or *siddur* ("ordering").

The rabbis determined the words, the time, the place, and even the pace of prayers. Wherever, whenever, and however disappeared.

For centuries, this arrangement was the glue that held the Jewish community together and became the focus of our spiritual life. Jews congregated in synagogue three times a day to pray. Organized prayer created a stable ritual amid the turmoil and uncertainty of Jewish living, and the words of the prayer book united us across time and place.

But we paid a steep price for this unity. While organized prayer successfully cohered the community, we lost the personal spontaneity and intimacy of prayer. Mouthing the scripted words became obligatory; *kavana* (personal intention) became optional. As order ruled, we stopped viewing prayer as a vehicle for emotional connection and personal transformation. No longer was prayer "work of the heart" (*avoda she'b'lev*), an intimate expression of our hearts and lives. After all, the human heart cannot be ordered or evoked on demand.

Thus began the shrinking of our prayer life. For two millennia, since the start of organized prayer, we have been equating our private, inner spiritual life with the public synagogue experience. Prayer shrunk from being a full, constant, and private expression of our souls to discrete, scheduled, and visible moments shared with the whole community. The rite of passage for entering the adult community—bar/bat mitzvah—meant learning how to lead communal prayers, not learning how to deepen a prayerful life or nurture a relationship with God. The emphasis on the external expression of our prayer came at the expense of our inner lives. We became literate in the words of the prayer book; we no longer needed to read the words of our hearts and souls.

For almost two thousand years we have sustained this very organized prayer routine.

The time has come to *dis-organize* our prayer life—to remind ourselves how to engage in a full and undivided prayerful life. It's time to step away from the set words and rituals just enough for our prayer to become a real conversation, with ourselves and with God.

This book asks:

- Can we bring our prayer life into the natural cycle of our living?

- Can our prayers become "words of the heart"—personal and intimate?

- Can we expand the scope of our prayer life beyond the walls of the synagogue?

- Can we break the routine of our prayer lives and renew our relationship with God?

- What would becoming a prayerful person look like for each of us?

- What are we seeking in our prayer life?

Once we may have been a prayerful people. The time has come to yearn, seek, and become prayerful individuals, and a prayerful people once again.

The Absence of Personal Heartfelt Conversations about Our Prayer Life

We are good at learning *about* prayer. We have countless books, articles, courses, and seminars talking *about* prayer. Several years ago I wrote a book *about* prayer.

This is not a book about prayer. It is not scholarly. There are no analyses of the words, thoughts, or ideas; there are no expositions on the history of prayers or their layers of interpretation.

Judaism calls prayer "work of the heart." Work of the heart needs words of the heart—words that emerge from a very deep, personal, and vulnerable place. That is what I offer here.

This is not a book from my head. These are reflections from my heart, from inside my prayer life.

I am more confident and secure when I talk from my head. It is my comfort zone—a place where I am in control. My children frequently say, "Abba (Dad) lives in his head." I come from a family of philosophers and scientists. To relax and totally let loose, I play chess. When talking from my heart, I feel exposed and vulnerable. Just contemplating opening up my inner life to potential scoffing or cynical reactions makes me queasy.

In my own world of prayer, it has been very challenging to let go of control. I continue to struggle to let down my intellectual guard and become more vulnerable in my relationship with God and prayer.

I have discovered that reflecting and writing are powerful triggers that jump-start my spiritual and prayer life. These activities invite me, compel me, to leave my comfort zone. For forty days I sat every morning and asked myself personal and penetrating questions about my prayer life—questions that challenged me, shook me up, and brought me to wrestle with the truth of my inner life.

What follows are ten of these questions from my heart about prayer. Though I offer my own personal reflections on these questions, I don't answer them. Why? These questions don't really have—perhaps should not have—answers. Once I answer a question, I am done with it. It no longer pursues me; I no longer carry it with me. But these are lifetime questions that should always be guiding my journey, reverberating within me.

I follow each question and reflection with my second take, exploring what triggered and inspired the initial response of my heart.

I offer all of these feelings and thoughts as a fellow traveler seeking to expand and intensify my own prayer experience and life. I hope they will encourage us to engage in a more sincere and transformative work of the heart, exploring new pathways of prayer on the journey to becoming more prayerful human beings.

Spiritual Harmonic Vibrations

I hope that sharing these reflections may resonate in a way that brings about harmonic vibrations. What are harmonic vibrations? If you arrange two guitars facing each other and pluck a string of one of the guitars, the corresponding string on the opposite guitar will begin to vibrate (without ever being touched!). This remarkable effect, wherein plucking the first string evokes a response in the corresponding string, is called harmonic vibration.

The same effect can be seen between human beings, often referred to as *attunement*. "Plucking" a string of our personality evokes a similar reaction in the people around us. If we pluck the cynical string, people around us tend to become more cynical. If we pluck a joyous, smiling string, it evokes a happy response in others.

I hope that plucking my work-of-the-heart string will evoke a similar response in you. You may begin to reflect on your prayer life—what it is now and what it could be. You may even want to share this feeling with others, giving them inspiration and courage to engage in heart-to-heart conversations about their prayer life.

It can be very difficult to deepen our prayer life if we are reluctant or self-conscious to talk about it. When was the last time you opened up your heart and spoke with a friend about the condition of your prayer life? We see a doctor annually for a physical checkup. We have the dentist check our teeth at least once a year. We even bring our cars to the garage for annual tests. When was the last time we had a prayer checkup?

How can we make sure we are maintaining our spiritual health if we don't examine how we are doing and consider the steps necessary for our personal growth?

Over the last number of years I have asked hundreds of people, of all ages, about their spiritual lives and their relationship with God. Almost every person remarked that they had never spoken with others about this part of their life. They were worried of being judged and regarded as strange.

It is time to remove the awkwardness and inhibition surrounding these conversations. We need to create space in which people feel comfortable reflecting on and talking about their prayer lives, their spiritual moments, and their personal relationships with God. We need the opportunity to talk from our hearts, even when we don't have clear and articulate answers.

II

HOW THIS BOOK WORKS

Each chapter is composed of three parts:

1. An original reflection
2. A commentary on the reflection
3. Trigger questions for further reflection and conversations

Original Reflection: Each reflection responds to a different question about prayer.

A Commentary on the Reflection: Often poems or reflections can be opaque, the message and ideas elusive. My commentary will hopefully unpack the reflections, making them more accessible and evocative. Writing these questions and reflections has pushed me to more deeply and personally engage the questions that surfaced in the original reflections, forcing me to do more work of the heart.

The artist Mark Rothko wrote that he hoped people would cry when seeing his paintings; he cried when he painted them.

I hope that people will not just read but also experience these reflections with their hearts; I wrote them from my heart.

Trigger Questions: The trigger questions are geared for friends, families, teachers, students—anyone who wants to grow in prayer. The questions are meant to start conversations, within yourself and with others, about how we can take the next steps in our prayerful life.

Growing up, I had no sense of God or personal prayer. I didn't know how to begin the conversation, and I would have been inhibited, self-conscious, and terrified if someone had asked me about my personal relationship with God. No one even offered to approach these issues. For decades, I missed out on nourishing my inner life and developing my own world of prayer.

Reflecting on this, I've realized that unless we actively push to open our souls and hearts, we may never have some of the most important conversations of our lives. How tragic is that?

We have souls, and we need to talk about our inner lives— even if we don't have clear answers, or if we spout clichés or contradict ourselves. It is not easy to be "clear" about something as elusive as one's soul and spiritual life.

I hope this book will create an inviting place to begin these personal and intimate conversations.

III

A DIFFERENT APPROACH TO PRAYER

Most people think that prayer is about saying the words in the prayer book. Or articulating a personal prayer. Or expressing gratitude. Some people look at prayer as an opportunity to connect with God—to enter a different spiritual zone.

They are all right. There are many faces of prayer. This book will touch on all these prayer types.

There is an additional approach to prayer that is quite different: not talking but listening. Listening to the prayer God is praying for us.

Through the inner voice of our soul, *God is constantly sending us the prayer we need to hear.* God is communicating to us. The Ba'al Shem Tov said that our soul talks to us. We hear this divine voice through our intuitions—sometimes gradually and sometimes suddenly, like a spiritual lightning bolt.

God sends each of us our own personal prayer, every day, all the time. We are not brought into this world for no reason, lost or abandoned. God is always whispering to us, conveying our particular role in the world. Each person has a unique prayer guiding his or her unique path. God begins this personal prayer at our birth, prior to our development of consciousness or ability to communicate.

This prayer exists independent of whether or not we hear it or articulate it. It has a life of its own. The mystics call it the soul of the universe. The prayer God sends us guides our steps as we continually create, direct, and heal God's beautiful and broken world.

God's prayer is always speaking to us, sending meaning, purpose, and direction. But we have to find the prayer. The first step in deepening our prayer life is pausing, listening, and being open to spiritual guidance. We may not be prophets, but each of us has a soul always communicating with us.

God created a world that is alive, in motion, and evolving to its next state of being. The soul of the world is yearning to become a bit more unified, a bit more healed, a bit more beautiful. As individuals, we are also in motion, yearning and evolving *into* our better selves while yearning and evolving *beyond* ourselves.

Prayer is the inner voice of the universe that beckons us to grow, to soulfully respond to the present needs of the world. It is always calling, whispering, singing, pleading, patiently befriending and encouraging us to journey another step on our path.

We do not create, utter, or spark our prayers. We pause and listen. We look for them. Sometimes we find them. And when we inevitably lose them, we need to pause, seek, and find them again.

1

WHAT IS PRAYER?

What is prayer?

A voice calling to us. A whisper.

"Hello. You are not lost in this world.
You are not wandering or drifting or drowning.
There is a special path for you. Just for you.

"Come. Take one more step.

"Don't be afraid.

"I will show you your path.
I have come into this world to speak just to you."

The path is always changing.
The prayer is always the same.

Always whispering:
"Friend. There is something missing.
Something broken in this world.
You have a piece. You have a thread. Help Me.
I need you to help Me.

"Listen. Be you. Look for your path."

THEMES

God is praying to us.

We are all called to a unique
path and role in healing this world.

Prayer invites us to take our next steps.

A voice calling to us.

It's so hard to listen.

I've never been a good listener. Listening does not come naturally for me. I like to talk, to be the center, to be active and in control. Growing up, at my parents' dining room table, we all spoke at the same time. I excelled in interrupting my sisters. It is difficult for me to be patient. I get annoyed with myself when I cut people off, but ... pausing and waiting is not my thing.

Looking back, it's really not surprising that my first moment of spiritual listening occurred against my will. I had never had a reflective or mindful practice. We did not talk about God or spirituality in my family. I had never tried to connect with anything holy or imagined I had a spiritual calling.

I was twenty-five years old, engaged to Sandra, and enrolled in a PhD program in clinical psychology. Becoming a psychologist seemed to be a very respectable direction, offering financial security and a bit of prestige. While talking with Sandra about how the next few years could unfold, a voice suddenly exploded within me—a voice of stunningly fierce determination and clarity. The voice proclaimed, "Listen. This psychology thing is not your path. Forget the degree. It's not you. You were born to be a teacher. Go into teaching."

I instantly became unsettled. Disoriented. Where was this idea coming from? How could I abandon such a clear and promising path as psychology? For teaching? Where was the prestige in that? Or the financial security? Plus, it would be a long road to get certified. I didn't even know where to look. Perhaps most unnerving, what would my parents and prospective in-laws say?

A voice calling to us. A whisper …
Come.
Don't be afraid.

I was terrified.

I had always been a dutiful and well-behaved kid. I obeyed my parents and wrote thank-you notes to my teachers. I tried to fit in. Even during the radical '60s and '70s I was never the independent one, never one to experiment. Now this voice was pushing me off my course. I was afraid … of everything.

Somehow, I listened to the voice. It was so pure and strong I felt I had little choice. Somehow, I grasped that to run away from the voice would have been running away from myself. To the great dismay of most who knew me, I left the clinical psychology program after one year. Becoming a teacher of Jewish studies was indeed a long road; over six years of study lay ahead of me.

Now, after almost four decades in education, I see that the whisper that so frazzled me and upset my life also led me to myself. It has not been a glamorous path. There have not been awards or prizes; not much job security or prestige either. But getting up each morning and sensing I am living what I was born to do is its own reward.

What is prayer?

I used to think that prayer began with me, when I opened my mouth and uttered the words. There are a lot of words to say in the prayer book. When I was focused and intentional, I would try to articulate the words clearly, slowly, and distinctly.

Now it seems to me that prayer begins with my ears. Prayer is not something we wish for. Prayer is something that wishes for us.

I start by listening. God has a particular prayer for me. The prayer:

> *"I will show you your path. I have come into this world to speak just to you."*

The most central question in our lives is "Why was I put on this earth?" We each have unique paths to be explored in our time here. There are countless good and respectable paths, but not every path is for us. The single and most daunting challenge in life is finding our own authentic path. How do I find it? How can I be certain I even have a path?

I didn't ask to be born. Certainly not into this body, with this DNA, to this family, generation, or place. Why? Is it all by chance, meaningless and random, or is it purposeful? How can I know?

I know by listening.

God has a prayer for us. Every time a child is born, a new prayer comes into the world. Each unique child's prayer begins whispering:

> *"Hello. You are not lost in this world.*
> *You are not wandering or drifting or drowning.*
> *There is a special path for you. Just for you."*

Years later, in my second decade of teaching, this inner voice once again whispered to me. I was no longer a kid starting out. Now I had a title: director of spiritual education. I had a good position, a promising career, and some financial security. But the voice whispered:

> *"It's time to leave. You are living an old script. Leave your job. Leave your secure salary, your title. It's time. You were not brought into this world to be stable and safe.*
>
> *There is more you should be doing. Get over it. Get going."*

Once again, I was stunned and terrified.

Only this time I didn't listen. I couldn't. Now the stakes were higher. I had six kids and a mortgage. Get going? To where exactly? I had held only one job my entire adult life and had achieved some measure of success. Plus, my self-image and self-esteem were wrapped up in my career. What exactly was I supposed to do?

The path is always changing.

The daring decision in my twenties to become a teacher did not mean that I had taken the final step on my path. That may have been the correct decision for my twenties. My fifties demanded a new step. I had exhausted the path of my earlier decision.

The prayer is always the same.

"Friend. There is something missing.
Something broken in this world.
You have a piece. You have a thread. Help Me.
I need you to help Me."

My inner voice was urging me: "Live the life the world needs from you. God created you, not as someone else's clone. You can do it. That's why you were brought into this world."

Once again I was faced with making a dramatic change in my life. The old script had been good for me. I had done well and knew that I could continue doing a good job, even if some of my passion and excitement had faded. I paused, heard the inner voice, and then continued on the old path. I just couldn't make the change. This time it was too scary.

For three years I ran away from my prayer. For three years, every day I told myself I couldn't do it. I refused to listen.

My prayer didn't let go. For three years, it kept whispering. It kept running after me: "Live the life the world needs from you."

I ran. It ran after me.

I ran and ran. I ran away from myself.

Did you ever not listen to your inner voice? Did you ever feel you were not living your life? There are few worse feelings in the world. The poet May Sarton writes:

Now I become myself. It's taken
Time, many years and places;
I have been dissolved and shaken,
Worn other people's faces.

I too have "worn other people's faces." When I think of other people's faces, I immediately flash back to my high school experience. I was an expert in other people's faces. I had to play on the football team (my father and grandfather played football). I had to sing in the choir (my mother's relatives were artists in Vienna). I had to wear bell-bottoms and grow my hair (it was the '70s). Wearing other people's faces was most of my life.

I didn't know I had a unique path. I didn't know that I had something unique to offer the world. I didn't even know that I was unique. Ordinary seemed closer to the truth. One look in the mirror told me that I was ordinary. I certainly didn't know that I was needed.

Prayer begins when we imagine, beyond any rational comprehension, that we are needed, that the world needs us. Prayer is about purpose in our lives.

There is a special path for you. Just for you.

God is whispering to me. Through my inner voice, my sense of intuition, my moment of connection, God is whispering for me to walk my path. The prayer is leading me to my path.

There is something missing.
Something broken in this world.

When we look around, it's not hard to notice that this world is not really such a great place to be. There are beautiful places and breathtaking moments, and sometimes we feel blessed. But for most people, most of the time, there is a lot of brokenness, sadness, disappointment, and unfairness.

I am born into a world that is, put simply, messed up. And so God prays to me:

> *"Friend. There is something missing.*
> *Something broken in this world.*
> *You have a piece. You have a thread. Help Me.*
> *I need you to help Me."*

When I stop and try to wear my face, I feel quite limited. What are my great gifts? What can I accomplish, really? I may be me, but am I worthy, special?

Then I remember: I have a prayer. I am needed.

"Listen. Be you. Look for your path."

It's all I really need to know about myself.

GUIDING QUESTIONS
FOR SELF-REFLECTION

What is prayer?

How would you answer this question?

How would you have answered this differently at another point in your life?

A voice calling to us. A whisper.

When have you had a moment, an intuition, when you felt guided from beyond?

How did you feel at that moment?

Looking back, how do you understand the experience now?

"Don't be afraid."

Were you ever afraid or reluctant to listen to your inner voice?

How did you overcome your fear to listen? What gave you the courage?

What advice would you give to someone who is reluctant or afraid to listen to the prayer of his or her soul?

The path is always changing. The prayer is always the same.

When have you been called to change your path?

How did it work out?

"Friend. There is something missing. Something broken in this world. You have a piece. You have a thread. Help Me. I need you to help Me."

How would you describe your "piece" to help heal or beautify the world?

When have you felt that God needed you?

2

HOW DID I LOSE MY PRAYER?

I lost my prayer.

I carried it for many years. Saying it every day.
Believing it less every day.
It withered and then was gone.

I didn't hear it fall. There was no squeak or twitch or "Oh."
My prayer silently wandered off, tired of the dulling routine.
Like a sailboat without wind, it drifted away.

My prayer knew I had given up on it. It had let me down.
Once a prayer full of yearning, vital and alive. Then an
angry prayer, impatient and threatening.

Finally, it was a "whatever" prayer, lifeless and empty.

Then it slipped through the cracks of my dried-up broken
heart and was gone.

What happens to lost prayers?

Do they float aimlessly? Wisps?
Do they mourn? Do they die?

Do they wander as orphans, cold, hungry, without a warm
embrace to call them home?
Do they reach out for a loving hand?

Is there a Lost & Found of abandoned prayers?

THEMES

Prayers losing vitality

Cycle of prayer life

I lost my prayer.

There is a natural cycle in the life of a prayer. Spring, summer, fall, winter. A cycle of life. Prayers too need to die. Their faded traces nurture new prayers.

Rav Abraham Isaac Kook writes of the cyclical nature of emotions. Like branches of a tree, emotions blossom, then lose their vitality, and eventually rebound—refreshed, stronger, and more beautiful.[1] The beauty of emotions is their dynamism and unpredictability. Prayers too.

I carried it for many years. Saying it every day.
Believing it less every day.
It withered and then was gone.

The words don't talk to me anymore. They stay on the page. I have said them too often. They once gave me a map to God. It doesn't work anymore. The words lead nowhere. The pages fall as leaves in the winter—crinkled, lifeless, dry.

I am crushed. I am ashamed. Embarrassed. Flooded with guilt. Who am I to stand in judgment of God's prayers? Once I bounced and swayed, rejoicing in every word, every letter— my body and soul leaping to the heavens. Delicious words—I remember so loving you.

I am left with stale memories. I tremble a great trembling (Genesis 27:33).

Is it my fault? Is it me? In synagogue, I stand alone. Stone cold. I have become the mannequin in the storefront. People walk by and mutter, "What happened to him?"

For so long, I prayed someone else's prayer. It was not the right fit. It was not the right voice. But I prayed it. I thought it was a good prayer. A nice prayer. The expected prayer.

It was just not my prayer. I have often prayed the prayer others wanted me to pray. Others smiled approvingly of the prayer. They expected me to pray it. I mouthed the words. They were like gravel in my throat.

It was a good prayer. A nice prayer. The expected prayer. It was just not my prayer.

I never knew that I had my own prayer. Why didn't they tell me?

My prayer knew I had given up on it.
It had let me down.
Once a prayer full of yearning, vital and alive.
Then an angry prayer, impatient and
   threatening.

Finally, it was a "whatever" prayer, lifeless and
   empty.

I have said the words too often. I have said them despite feeling disconnected from them. Too often. Practice and practice of saying the words while not being in the words has left me empty. A routine that drained and killed itself.

I am lost. And lonely. And afraid. When my prayer becomes "lifeless and empty," I become untethered. Drifting aimlessly. I sense that I have silently departed from myself; I am living a short distance from myself.[2] A state of spiritual exile.

Is there a Lost & Found for lost people? Without my prayer I wander around the universe. Walking, breathing, smiling, but floating aimlessly.

In the desert, clouds of glory guided a wandering people. Where is my tiny wisp? In the desert, columns of fire guided six hundred thousand. Where is my tiny spark?

What happens to lost prayers?

Have I lost my prayer? I don't know what my next steps are. I don't hear my inner voice. I trudge on.

Voices ping-pong in my head:

Maybe I need a break.

Maybe I have searched for so long that I just can't continue right now.

Maybe my searching for God has left me traumatized.

Maybe I justify my not searching by saying I need a break.

Maybe life comes in cycles of journeying and resting, of losing and finding.

Maybe I'm just lazy and too easy on myself.

I'm left exhausted and confused.
Have you ever lost your prayer?

Is there a Lost & Found of abandoned prayers?

What happens to prayers at the Lost & Found? They sit and
wait, their number not called. What do prayers do while waiting? Are they impatient? Do they shrivel up? Do they cry? Or
sing? Or raise their voice and scream? Do they run in place?
Do they look down, dejected? Rejected? Forlorn? Do they die?
Are they passed on?

I think they wait. And know. And smile.

My lost prayer did not forget me. It is waiting for me. It is
still calling. What will it be when it wanders back? When the
wind picks up? Will I recognize its voice? Will a patient God
gently escort my prayer back to me? Will I open my arms and
cry? Will I smile a tiny wink with my lips, saying, "I know
you"? Will I look at it as an old friend with whom there are no
secrets? Will I apologize?

"I'm sorry I let you down."

"Yes, I thought something was missing."

"Yes, I barely carried on without you."

It's a mysterious journey, losing and finding our prayers.
Our prayer is seeking us, waiting for us. Loving us, it waits to
be found.

I have to learn how to pray again.

GUIDING QUESTIONS
FOR SELF-REFLECTION

I lost my prayer.

When have you felt angry or impatient in your prayer life?

When have you felt spiritually empty?

My prayer knew I had given up on it.
It had let me down.
Once a prayer full of yearning, vital and alive.
Then an angry prayer, impatient and threatening.
Finally, it was a "whatever" prayer,
lifeless and empty.

When have you felt ashamed or guilty about your prayer life?

Why did you feel ashamed or guilty? For example, was it the prayer book? Was it what was going on in your life?

What happens to lost prayers?

How did you recover your prayer life?

Looking back, do you think your spiritual crisis might have helped build you?

Is there a Lost & Found of abandoned prayers?

Do you feel more lost or found in your prayer life?

What do you do to regain your spiritual center?

What helps you become more connected to your prayer life?

What piece of advice would you give to yourself to help you take the next step in your prayer life?

3

WHAT IS MY PRAYER—RIGHT NOW?

Everything in my life has brought me to today's prayer.

*Today may not be the most spectacular or memorable day
    of my life,
but it's the most important.
Everything has led up to today.*

*Yesterday's prayer might have been majestic and dramatic.
But it died at sundown.*

*Every day has its own prayer.
Every day, a new prayer is searching for us.
Every day, a new prayer is born.*

*Today God composed a new prayer for me.
Whispering it now.*

*My prayer today will only happen once. Only today.
How would I treat a friend who only visits once in
    my lifetime?*

*Memo to myself:
"Open yourself up to today's prayer.
Don't miss it.
Don't lose it.
Go find it.*

*Dare to change.
Dare to be changed."*

THEMES

Living the prayer of today

Waking up to the present moment

Celebrating today's spiritual message

Letting go of control

Everything in my life has brought me to today's prayer.

It's easy to mistake today for yesterday. They look so much alike. It's easy to think they are the same. They're not. Neither physically nor spiritually. Today is not a repeat of yesterday. But so often we pray the same way today as we did yesterday. What if we are so busy hearing yesterday's prayer that we miss the prayer of today?

It's really hard to hear today's prayer, while I am so attached to yesterday. I love yesterday. It's known, familiar. It's become part of me. It's mine, I have a history with it.

And yesterday's yesterday? It's full of memories. My memories. I own it.

And the yesterday of yesterday's yesterday? Full of nostalgia. Tugging at my heart.

But today? Who owns today? Who is in control of "later on"? I don't own it. I have no idea what it will be.

I create the illusion of being in control by making schedules. I love making to-do lists. They make me feel busy, worthy, needed. When I ask friends how they are doing, I usually hear back, "Busy. So much going on." I don't think I've ever heard someone say, "I've got lots of time on my hands. Not much going on."

I confess that I am a bit of a control freak. I once criticized the font in an employee's report. There are a bunch of classes I've given dozens of times—my set of canned public lectures. They work. I know exactly where to put the jokes and stories, when to pause for dramatic effect, and precisely when to deliver the epic conclusion. I like being in control. It relieves a lot of stress and uncertainty for me. "Spontaneity" is a word in a foreign language.

The unfortunate thing is that none of us are really in control. It's an illusion, which precludes potential growth.

One day last year I got out of bed, raring to go. Healthy and feeling great. A full day planned ahead. Then—*pow!*—pain in my stomach had me reeling. Kidney stone. They say it's more painful than birthing twins naturally. (Well … almost.)

I'm in control? Really? Of what? I have no idea what is going on inside my body—then or now. I need a big dose of humility.

Am I in control of my spiritual life? Do I control God? *Taking control* of my spiritual life begins with me *letting go of control* of my spiritual life. I can't let myself *be controlled* by my need to control. I need to take a deep breath and ask:

What will today offer?

A new plan? A new hope?

A detour on my path?

Is a new thought on its way?

A new prayer?

Everything in my life has brought me to today's prayer.

It seems to me that some people are more alive than others. Why is that? Is it their metabolism? Their genetic disposition? The love they received as children? What would my life look like if I were totally crazy insanely awake and alive?

Maybe some people are more alive because they are more open to what today may offer.

Maybe, just maybe, they are more open to listening to a new prayer. I want that too.

Yesterday's prayer might have been majestic and dramatic.
But it died at sundown.

Lifeless prayers. Soulless prayers. Mouths moving. Hearts not. What happens when the words are not connected to the heart?

Air floating. Letters falling to the ground like stones. Sometimes in synagogue I feel buried under an avalanche of stones.

Prayer is meant to disrupt the routine of life. To shake us up and refocus us. It is not meant to become a new routine. When prayer becomes routine, it is prayer in name only—a body without a soul. Even creative personal prayer can turn into a routine if one is praying the same personal prayer every day.

What would happen if there were a rule that every evening in synagogue we had to pause and wait for a new thought, a new connection, or a new hope that we had never prayed before? Would the air be different? Would the words be like bouquets of blossoming flowers? Would the synagogue have a different fragrance?

Every day has its own prayer.
Every day, a new prayer is searching for us.

Every day, a new prayer is born.

Today God composed a new prayer for me.
Whispering it now.

What is my prayer—today? Will I hear my prayer today?

I know I can plan out a good day. I know I can do most things on my to-do list. I know I can achieve a lot. But will it be a prayerful day? Will it be the day my soul designed for me, is asking of me?

Am I open to surprise and the unknown? Or will I work to stay busy enough to avoid any disruption to my schedule?

Am I overplanning my life? Am I terrified of losing control? Am I not leaving any space for God?

Am I blabbing nonstop? Never pausing to ask God, "Do you have anything You'd like to say? Anything at all? Please. Speak up."

Sometimes I wish God's prayer was less polite. Interrupt me. Talk louder. Shut me up so I can hear You. What's the plan?

Well-mannered prayers are so easy to ignore.

Memo to myself:
"Open yourself up to today's prayer.
Don't miss it.
Don't lose it.
Go find it.
Dare to change.
Dare to be changed."

I love old scripts. Judaism has a tradition of old scripts. We call them customs. Some are hundreds of years old; some are new.

In our home, my wife and I have developed new family customs:

> At our Friday night meal we share a highlight from the week.

> At Havdala (the "closing ceremony" of Shabbat) we all share a moment from Shabbat we want to bring into the week.

> We have mustard herring for Shabbat morning Kiddush.

> At the Passover Seder, we use artichokes for karpas (bitter herb).

We're very attached to customs, especially the ones we've created. Maybe even a bit addicted to them. We could never let them slide. And yet . . .

Maybe God wants to share a new and different revelation with me today. Could I fit that into my schedule? Or am I so set on my schedule, customs, and routine, so wed to the words I am used to saying, that I am putting God's prayer on call-waiting?

Today, a new prayer is entering my soul. Am I recycling yesterday's message? Am I addicted to "same-old, same-old"? Do I dare to change? I don't want to be a stranger to my own soul.

GUIDING QUESTIONS
FOR SELF-REFLECTION

Today's prayer.

What is today's prayer for you?

When have you prayed yesterday's prayer?

What spiritual scripts are you ready to let go of?

Everything in my life has brought me to today's prayer

When have you brought your whole life—strengths and weaknesses, victories and defeats—to your prayer life?

When have you avoided bringing your whole life—strengths and weaknesses, victories and defeats—to your prayer life?

Yesterday's prayer might have been majestic and dramatic.
But it died at sundown.

When have you prayed a new prayer?

How was that for you?

Every day has its own prayer.
Every day, a new prayer is searching for us.
Every day, a new prayer is born.

Today God composed a new prayer for me.
Whispering it now.

How do you make space for God in your life?

What piece of advice would you give to yourself to make more room for God?

Memo to myself:
"Open yourself up to today's prayer.
Don't miss it.
Don't lose it.
Go find it.
Dare to change.
Dare to be changed."

Have you ever created a new practice or custom that was hard to let go? How was that for you?

What does "Dare to change / Dare to be changed" bring up for you?

4

WHAT AM I PRAYING FOR?

Hiraeth

The Welsh word for deep yearning for something lost.

A longing, nostalgia, and dreaming for a life
that you can never return to,
or maybe never was.

A home destroyed. A country lost. A childhood memory.
A time that plucks the inner chord of your being and will
    never let go.
Wherever you are—
Hiraeth.

You see the trees, the mountains, smell the air. But not quite.
You cannot stop yourself, you know it will break your heart,
and still you long for it.
Never reaching. Sweet. Unbearable.

A homesickness that will never be resolved.
The only place you belong. The only place you will never be.

Like Moses, gazing toward the Promised Land.

The Welsh say it is a longing to be where your soul lives.

We too are homesick.
Our hearts are longing, pulsing with an elusive hope
    and sadness.

We too are yearning.

But not for our past.
We are yearning for our future.

For that better world that is always coming,
    always coming.
We live in almost.

Hiraeth.

For our future home that we may never see.
It is where our soul lives.

THEMES

Yearning *as the home of our soul*

Brokenness *of the present moment*

Homesickness *for the future*

Hiraeth.

What is your *hiraeth*? For what would you be willing to give up everything? Even to have for just one moment?

My sister gave me a nickname when I was three years old: Bing. No one knows why, but it stuck. From then on, my father and uncle always called me Bing. Even after I got married and had kids, I was always Bing to my father and uncle.

There is something very precious about a nickname. It's not the name everyone calls you. Not the name on your driver's license or passport. It's a name born from a relationship. Whenever my father or uncle called me Bing, it was more than a name. It was cute and silly and just ours; calling out to play the three-year-year old boy within the grown man. It was love. It was intimate. It was always said with a twinkle and laugh. A joke between us, for over fifty years.

My uncle passed away seven years ago. My father, four years ago. Now there is no one to call me Bing. The name has died. A part of me has disappeared forever. I miss it terribly. *Hiraeth.*

Yearning.

Prayer. It's all about the yearning.

The poet Mary Oliver unknowingly, beautifully, tapped into profound Jewish wisdom: "Listen, are you breathing just a little, and calling it a life?"[3]

In the wise Hebrew language, there is one shared word for breathing and yearning: *she'ifa*. What gives me life? Breathing. What gives me life? Yearning.

No breathing—no life. No yearning—no life.

Are you breathing just a little? Are you yearning just a little? Are you living just a little? Yearning makes a life worth living. Yearning—living in the state of "What if?" and "Perhaps." An unknown world. A world of dreams and imagining.

Prayer is a rejection of the now. I think if God sends us only one prayer it is: "It can be different."

How can I make today different? What am I being called to do? Now? What am I yearning for? What does a deep breath of yearning feel like? Where is my "What if?" Where is my "Perhaps"?

Prayer is not meant to be quiet or calm. We need to banish decorum from our prayers. There is no order to follow. No page to turn. No ritual. Prayer is not a ceremony, not a service.

Prayer is a scream: "It can be different." Am I yearning to hear my prayer?

I need to take a deep breath of yearning. I need to live a little bit more.

A homesickness that will never be resolved.
The only place you belong. The only place you
    will never be.

Like Moses, gazing toward the Promised Land.

Rav Abraham Isaac Kook writes that each of the forefathers
imprinted a quality on our soul.[4] Abraham gave us kindness.
Isaac gave us courage. Jacob gave us truth.

Moses gave us yearning. The reluctant leader, who
dedicated his life to bringing a people to the Promised
Land, never stepped foot in the Land. Moses was brought
to the border to gaze longingly. Moses lived in "almost." He
bequeathed this image to us and imprinted it on the Jewish
soul: a spiritual DNA of "almost," of yearning.

We are yearning for our future. For that better
    world that is always coming.

When we meet someone, the most common questions asked
are "Where are you from? What do you do?" But the most
meaningful and revealing questions would be "Where are you
going? What are you yearning for?"

We are more the product of our future than our past.
What are your hopes? Your aspirations? What is the title of
the next chapter in the book of your life?

Prayer is a call to the future. Prayer is a protest movement.
A demonstration against the present.

Often we hear today the spiritual language of "living
in the moment," "becoming fully present in the moment,"

"accepting and embracing reality." The promise of contentment and inner peace entices us.

Prayer is a shriek of unacceptance: I don't accept the world as it is right now!

Yes, it is all a gift.

Yes, I am grateful beyond words.

Yes, God is a generous and benevolent creator.

But it's not good enough. I want the better world that is always coming. I have a role to play in bringing us closer to that better world.

I don't want to live only in this moment; I want to live in the past, present, and future moments.

I don't want to live fully in the beauty of this moment; I want to live fully in the brokenness of the moment.

Yes, I know I am kvetching. I am screaming to God that this world, so mercifully created, so blessed to live in, is not good enough. I am breathing and yearning for a world that is a drop better. *Hiraeth.*

And you know what? God agrees.

They say that as a young boy, Mozart had a hard time getting out of bed. His mother would play a discordant chord on the piano. He had no choice but to rise to resolve the dissonance.

God plays a lot of discordant chords for us. Prayer is our chance to hear them. It's time for us to get up.

GUIDING QUESTIONS
FOR SELF-REFLECTION

Hiraeth

What is your *hiraeth*? Your yearning?

How does your yearning express itself in your prayer life?

> *A homesickness that will never be resolved.*
> *The only place you belong.*
> *The only place you will never be.*

> *Like Moses, gazing toward the Promised Land.*

What advice would you give yourself to deepen your sense of yearning?

What is your Promised Land that you can only gaze at?

How do you balance the desire for contentment and inner peace with yearning?

For that better world that is always coming,
always coming.

Which discordant chords in life wake you up? Stir you to action?

Hiraeth.
For our future home that we may never see.
It is where our soul lives.

Where would you say your soul lives?

.

5

HOW AM I DOING WITH GOD?

At first, God came into my life as an unwanted guest.

Unwanted and uninvited.

At first, I thought the guest never stopped talking,
never stopped making demands,
and never stopped judging me.

After some time I noticed that the guest was silently listening.
The guest sat there, listening to me so deeply that I began to
    listen to myself.
And it was my voice doing the talking, making the demands,
    and judging.

Finally, I had enough. Politely, I asked my guest to leave.
I nudged the guest toward the door. The guest left.

Years later, I needed the guest.
I was ready for the guest to return.
The guest was wanted and invited.
My home was empty. My voice unhearable.
How could I listen to myself without the guest?

It took me way too long to realize that I had it all backward.
I was a guest in God's home. Wanted and invited.

Now it's my turn to listen.

THEMES

Bringing God into our lives

Discomfort and challenge of a relationship with God

Running away from God / running to God

At first, God came into my life as an
*   unwanted guest.*

This is the hardest chapter to write. Even after all these years, I'm still uncomfortable talking about my relationship with God. A relationship with God is so personal. With whom can I share it?

    Plus, my own relationship with God is so embarrassing. A mixture of clichés, theological proclamations worthy of a third grader, and contradictions. How could I tell anyone? What would they think of me?

God walks into my life and a tumult of thoughts cascade in my head:

    If I do kind acts, will good things happen to me?

    I know that bad things happen to good people.

    Can I believe both of these at the same time?
    Did I just contradict myself?

    What do you want from me? Am I good enough?

    Do you really exist, or are you a projection of my psyche?

    Where have you been? A lot of people have
    been depending on you and it seems that you
    (You?) just took some time off.

I don't need you.

I'm lost without you.

I pause to catch my breath.

God sits and waits.

I continue, "Well? Show me your stuff. Let's see a miracle. Lightning or thunder or a baby earthquake. Or something closer to home, such as making the cancer of my friend's daughter disappear. Or my student's mental illness vanish. I'd even settle for my hearing to stop deteriorating. You're the creator of the world, give me something."

God sits and waits.

These conversations are so hard for me. Growing up, my family never spoke about God. In all of my childhood I can only remember one sentence uttered. My Aunt Liza—who taught at MIT for fifty years, should have won a Nobel Prize, and is considered the resident genius of our family—once remarked, "God is the greatest thing that man ever created." And that was that. No one else dared say anything. End of conversation.

When I meet Aunt Liza now she offers me this silent quizzical look, as if to say, "Wow. Aryeh. It is so interesting to see someone like you. We thought people like you died out in the Middle Ages."

When I was in college, my father once asked me to run the family Passover Seder. I agreed, on the condition that I could eliminate every reference to God. We finished Seder in eight minutes.

So now I'm lost. I don't even know what I don't know. Do I believe in God? And what does that mean?

Unwanted and uninvited.

At a very confused stage of my life, otherwise known as my twenties, I spent a few weeks in the Old City of Jerusalem. I was wrestling with this Jewish thing: belief / people / Torah / truth / Israel. It was all new for me, and it shook me up.

At one point I needed to clear my head. With no destination in mind, I started walking. Within moments, I was lost in the cobblestone maze of the Old City.

I turned a corner and bumped into an elderly man. I was about to carry on, but something about him caught my eye. He looked vaguely familiar. Yes, I had met him once before. "You're a rabbi, right? You're my rabbi's rabbi?"

He had no idea who I was. "Yes, I'm a rabbi. Who are you?"

"Three months ago, before I left for Israel, my synagogue honored me with a special Friday night service and you were there visiting my rabbi, your student."

"Yes, I remember."

"What are you doing now?" I asked him.

"Well, I was visiting Israel, but I got an urgent message this morning that my sister had taken ill, and I have to make an emergency return trip to the US. Since my trip is getting cut short, I wanted to visit the Kotel one last time. I came to the Old City, but now I'm completely lost."

Two people getting lost. At the same time. At the same place. Turning a corner. Random?

Two people who met once. By chance?

"Do you mind if I ask you a question?" I said.

I asked the question about God that I had spinning in my head thirty minutes before.

His answer shocked me. I can quote it verbatim today, forty years later. His words about God and Torah changed my life.

We said goodbye, and we each went back to trying to find our way.

God, was that you? Did you invite yourself into my life? Were you being sneaky? Did you have a plan?

Uninvited.

Not long ago I was asked to lead a Friday night experience for a group of Birthright Israel participants. Three options for services were offered: traditional, progressive, and not interested. I took the thirty participants who chose "not interested."

We sat in a circle. I asked everyone to turn to the person next to them and share a spiritual moment they had this week. Everyone turned and shared. Then I asked them to turn in the other direction and share one quality of theirs they would deem spiritual. Again, everyone shared. No pushback or rolling eyes.

Then I took a risk. I asked everyone to stand up. I said that in a moment we were going to walk around the large hotel ballroom and talk directly to God. What would we talk about? I said I would like everyone to complete this sentence: "Dear God, it's been a while since we've talked, but this is what is on my mind ..."

Just walk and talk. For five minutes.

I gathered everyone together after the five minutes and asked how it was. The first person said it was strange to talk aloud. The next person also said it was weird and different. But when the third person said that "it was not enough time," virtually everyone raised their hand in agreement. They said it was the first time in their lives they had ever talked to God in their own words.

It must be hard to be God, so rarely invited to the conversation.

The guest sat there, listening to me so deeply that
I began to listen to myself.
And it was my voice doing the talking, making
the demands, and judging.

It was during my yeshiva days that I ran headfirst into anxiety and guilt. I loved studying Jewish law. I kept telling myself, "God is in the details." Mountains of details. How should I open a tuna fish can on Shabbat? Can I straighten out this picture frame? Did I daydream during *psukei d'zimra*? Read *mishnayot* while waiting for the bus—don't waste a moment! Can I read this children's book to my kids, or will it discourage holiness? There was not a moment in the day when the voice in my head didn't clamor and judge.

Was I living for holiness? Or was I living on trial? I was the accused, never living an innocent day.

Constantly judging myself led me to judge others. Endless comparing, endless scrutiny. Endless insecurity and disappointment.

My God was a god of Jewish law, judgment, endless details. In yeshiva, we never talked about God. We never discussed our personal relationships with God. The only question we asked: What does God demand from me?

Finally, I had enough. Politely, I asked my guest
  to leave.
I nudged the guest toward the door.
The guest left.

I had to find a new God. Not the God of judgment. Not a God of books. I had to find a personal God, one in whose image I would want to live. I had no idea how to do that.

The hardest part of my journey has been spiritual loneliness. Often I felt stranded on an island of purgatory. I couldn't talk to the rabbis I knew; they would either not understand or judge me harshly. I couldn't talk to my friends; this was way too personal and vulnerable. And most of the time I couldn't even talk about it to myself. I had moved thousands of miles away from home, changed my life, and was the head of a family—how could I reconsider my decisions?

It took me way too long to realize that I had it
  all backward.
I was a guest in God's home.
Wanted and invited.

Now it's my turn to listen.

It took me way too long to realize that I don't know anything about God.

During my first year of teaching, one of my students asked to speak with me privately. We were in the third month of the year, and so far she had been a model student. About twenty-five years old, with a background in theater and trained in learning scripts, she would memorize the texts we were opening in the Beit Midrash. Though she came from very little Jewish background, one could feel her glowing during every moment of learning. We sat outside and she told me that she needed to leave—to go back home. I was totally startled.

"But you seem to love what you're doing. Why do you need to leave?"

"I miss my family. I really need to be with them."

"Where is your family? Where will you be?"

"My family is in Arizona. I'll be going to Boston."

Long pause. Then she starts again. "It's not really my family. I need to get on with my life. To start my PhD."

"Your program is a long one. Five years. Does it make such a difference if you start in January or September?"

Long pause. It was my first year of teaching and I had no idea what was going on with her.

Then she burst into tears and said, "I have to go. This God thing is so new and scary for me. I'm afraid of losing myself if I stay."

I didn't know what to say. She left the program.

Many, many years later, I can echo her thoughts. This God thing is actually quite scary, and I don't know what will happen to me if I stay. But I'm no longer afraid of losing myself. In fact, I think the opposite is true—I'm finding myself.

Realizing that I don't know anything has enabled me to be more accepting of my clichés and contradictions. If that sounds like a third grader, I'm okay with that now.

GUIDING QUESTIONS
FOR SELF-REFLECTION

At first, God came into my life as an unwanted guest

How would you describe your relationship with God?

Why do you think it is so difficult to talk about a personal relationship with God?

How would you describe your level of satisfaction with your relationship with God today? What would you like to change?

> *The guest sat there, listening so deeply that I began to hear myself.*

> *And it was my voice doing the talking, making the demands, and judging.*

What qualities, moods, or reactions does your relationship with God evoke in you?

Finally, I had enough. Politely, I asked my guest to leave.

I nudged my guest toward the door. The guest left.

When have you nudged God out the door of your life? What happened?

When have you felt the absence of God in your life?

It took me way too long to realize that I had it all backward.

I was a guest in God's home. Wanted and invited.

Now it's my turn to listen.

How do you invite God into your life?

Do you believe any contradictory ideas about God? How do you feel about that?

How has your relationship with God helped you to lose or find yourself?

6

WHO CAN HELP ME PRAY?

What would happen if we renamed the synagogue
  "The Lost & Found of Prayers"?

Everyone would come in and look for the prayer
  they had lost.
They would read the labels on each prayer, finding their own.

Do they even know they have lost their prayer?

Who is the Master of Prayer?

The one who prays for everyone to remember
  they have lost their prayer.
The one who wakes us up to look for it.

The one who prays: "Please, God, let me help everyone find
  the prayer they have lost."

Be a Master of Prayer. Pray hard for your friends.

THEMES

Going through the motions of prayer

Spiritual listening

A new approach to the *Ba'al Tefila* (prayer leader)

What would happen if we renamed the
    synagogue "The Lost & Found of Prayers"?

Everyone would come in and look for the prayer
    they had lost.

They would read the labels on each prayer,
    finding their own.

Do they even know they have lost their prayer?

It is so easy to go through the motions of prayer. It is so easy to enter the synagogue, pick up the prayer book, and say the words. It is so easy to be an obedient pray-er.

    Should prayer really be so easy?

For three years I ran away from my prayer. It kept running after me. I was scared.

    My prayer persisted, whispering, "It's time to leave. You are living an old script. Leave your job. Leave your secure salary, your title. It's time. You were not brought into this world just to be stable and safe. There is more you should be doing. Get over it. Get going."

    I couldn't get going. So I ran away. I ran away from myself.

    Did you ever not listen to your inner voice? Did you ever feel you were not living your life?

For three years, every day, I told myself I couldn't do it. Then, a friend—while walking out of my office, gathering coffee cups, and turning out the light—tossed an offhand comment: "You really could do more. You should believe in yourself more. Why are you hesitating? You can do it."

How did he know my prayer?

In a moment, I stopped running away. I drowned the fear and doubt. I left my job to start my new path.

Is your friend looking for his or her prayer? Sometimes it is very close.

We pray alone. Standing, silent. But next to others. Alone, but not alone.

Sometimes the prayer of your friends is just behind them. Gently turn them around. Hold them with both hands. Reach out their hands until the prayer lands on their fingertips. Hot as fire. Light as a cloud.

Sometimes our prayers are so close by. We just need a friend to turn us around. The best friend is someone who brings us to hear our own prayer.

Who is the Master of Prayer?

The one who prays for everyone to remember
    they have lost their prayer.
The one who wakes us up to look for it.

Who is the Master of Prayer? Should this person be the one with the beautiful voice, fluent in leading the prayer service? Or should this person be our spiritual leader?

Who is our spiritual leader today? For centuries, our spiritual leaders were the ones with the largest quantity of knowledge, the ones with the answers.

Not long ago I gave a rabbi a ride. During our conversation I began to harangue parts of our community, including the predictable behavior of many of our religious leaders. I ranted, "You know what really bothers me about rabbis? Whatever the question is, they always have the answer. They always think they know everything and immediately offer a solution."

Without missing a beat, he responded, "I'll tell you exactly why that is."

Do spiritual leaders have all the answers? Does *anyone* always have the answer?

It would have helped me if he had listened a bit more, instead of straightaway giving his answer.

Why is the Master of Prayer (*Ba'al Tefila*) the one who talks? Why is the Master of Prayer the one who knows how to say the prayers? Sing the songs? What would happen if the Master of Prayer was the one who listened instead of talked?

What would happen if the Master of Prayer was the one who evoked our prayers? Spoke our inner language?

What would happen if the Master of Prayer was the curator of our souls? Led us to our spiritual lives?

I have found that I am a different person in the presence of three specific friends. With them I find a deeper and more articulate side of myself. But *only* with these three friends.

What do they do? They listen deeply.

When someone listens deeply to me, I begin to listen deeply to myself. I discover a new part of myself. They bring me to hearing my story, my soul.

I think there is a simple test of spiritual awareness:

Does the person ask a follow-up question, or turn the conversation to him/herself?

Does the person answer you, or help you find your own answer?

What would happen if the Master of Prayer was that deep listener for all of us? What would happen if our community prioritized, valued, and trained deep listeners? What if we trained kids coming through their rite of passage to adulthood (bar/bat mitzvah) how to listen deeply? How to evoke a soul?

A friend once asked me for advice on how he could become a better listener. I suggested that he try loving people more. When you love someone, you can listen for hours. When you don't like someone, it's really hard to listen.

What if our communal rite of passage was a training in loving, listening, and evoking souls? What if we learned how to ask follow-up questions and listen deeply for the questions that others have but are not asking? What if our kids did apprenticeships in listening and learned how to listen deeply to people of all ages?

What if the Masters of Prayer (and those in training to become Masters of Prayer) became the models of loving, listening, and evoking?

I don't think I could become a Master of Prayer for my community, nor for many people. But perhaps I could become a Master of Prayer for a few. Maybe even for just one.

It starts with listening—safe, generous listening, without

judgment or self-centered curiosity. It starts with a question: "When was your moment?"

When was the moment you heard your prayer?

When was the moment you felt God speaking to you?

When was the moment that shifted your life?

What color was the sky?

What shoes were you wearing?

What happened before? After?

Was anyone with you?

Were you sitting or standing?

Was there a dog barking in the background?

Did you know it at the time?

Can you feel it now?

Have you ever talked to anyone about your moment? Talk to me. I want to feel your moment. I want to touch it. I want to be there with you.

Tell me yours, and I'll tell you mine.

I'm so tired of making conversation. I'm so tired of talking on the surface of life. Tell me your moment. Don't be afraid. I will guard it. Protect it. Treasure it. Revere it. I'll never drop it.

Would you like to hear about mine?

I was sitting cross-legged under a eucalyptus tree in South-ern California. It was the Fourth of July. Kids were playing baseball nearby. I was wearing leather sandals and a flannel shirt. My friend had blonde hair and blue eyes. She listened intently. And I told her …

Maybe I'll never be a *Master* of Prayer. But maybe I could become a friend who believes you have a prayer, who helps you find your own prayer.

Be a master of prayer. Pray hard for your friends.

If I could only offer one piece of advice to the world, it would be this: find the friend who will journey with you.

Abraham had Sara. Moses had Aaron. Naomi had Ruth.

It's just too hard to journey alone.

GUIDING QUESTIONS
FOR SELF-REFLECTION

———————

*What would happen if we renamed the synagogue
"The Lost & Found of Prayers"?*

When have you felt you lost your prayer?

When have you felt you found your prayer?

**How did you find your prayer, and who helped you? How
did they help?**

Who is the Master of Prayer?

*The one who prays for everyone to remember they
have lost their prayer.
The one who wakes us up to look for it.*

**What do you think should be the qualities of a Master of
Prayer?**

**How could you pray for others to find their soul? What
would be your words?**

**How good of a listener are you? What advice would you
give yourself to become a better listener?**

Be a Master of Prayer. Pray hard for your friends.

Who is the friend you could journey with?

Who needs you to reach out and help them journey?

7

WHAT CAN PRAYER DO?

Prayer is the "work of the heart."[5]

Every day we wake up and harden our hearts a little bit.
We say to ourselves:

Today—I want to be in control.
Today—I want to succeed.
Today—is my day.

And then our day begins:

A mean boss.
A nasty driver.
An unanswered email.

And life hardens our hearts a little bit more.

Pharaoh had a hard heart. A heart giving life only to him.

Nothing got into Pharaoh's heart.
Not words or actions or God.
How can God enter a hard heart?

A trace of Pharaoh's hard heart pulses within me, every day.

Every day I wake up and think,
"What will be good for me today?"

And then comes prayer—the work of the heart.

How can I soften my heart?
How can I let others in?
How can I let God in?

And so I work on it. I do the work of the heart.

I pray for the strength to soften my heart.
I pray for the wisdom and will and love to listen to the
 prayer God is praying for me.

I pray with all of my heart for God to open my heart.
Prayer is such hard work.

THEMES

Emotional transformation of prayer

The hard work of softening our heart

Praying and becoming a loving person

Prayer is the "work of the heart."

Prayer is work. Hard work.

Showing up and saying the words is not work. Singing the songs and becoming emotionally uplifted is not work. Spiritual connection is not work.

Work is demanding. Work is exhausting. Work is transformative. Work brings about change: "I'm working on the garden. I'm working on an idea. I'm working on a relationship."

People ask me, "How's the book going?" I answer, "I'm working on it."

Prayer is the work of the heart. I am working to change my heart. And my heart affects everything else.

What could be harder and more demanding than that?

"'And you will work for God with all of your heart.' What is the work of the heart? Prayer" (Babylonian Talmud, Ta'anit 2a).

"You will love God with *all* of your heart, with *all* of your soul, and with *all* of your might" (Deuteronomy 6:5).

That's a lot of *alls*. An "everything" prayer. How does an "everything" prayer look?

Whatever it is, I don't think I'm doing it.

Too much for me.

Too much heart.

Too much soul.

Too much might.

I'm sorry, God. You thought I could do it. You called me to *all*. I'll give you *some*.

Did you really think I could give you all? I don't think I am an *all* person. I am a *some* person. Sometimes maybe even an *a lot* person. But not an *all* person.

How does one become an *all* person? There are parts of *not all* that stick like gum to the bottom of my shoe. How do you scrape off the *not all* parts?

How does a *some* person become an *all* person?

How can I soften my heart?
How can I let others in?

Last year, for a short time, I heard my prayer. I listened to my inner voice. For a few moments, I stopped being afraid. I journeyed with it. I let my prayer transform my heart.

Something happened to me when I began to hear my prayer. I found my better self.

Unplanned, unintentional, and to my surprise, I began to deeply feel the brokenness of others. I didn't know how to explain this to myself. I had never been especially kind before.

I wrote to Michael. And Steven. And Stuart. I could not *not* write. I planned a trip to comfort Rina during her *shiva*, though normally I wince at those kinds of visits. I felt their pain acutely. I found that listening came easily. I was there for them. Fully, without effort. I began to anticipate what my friends needed. I didn't need to think about their pain—I felt it.

Often I wonder, with all the clear needs in the world, with

all the blatant injustice and pain and tears in the world, why am I talking about prayer? Am I wasting my time? But finding my prayer turned out not to be self-absorbed at all. Working on my heart was the best thing I could do for others.

Last year, for a few moments, I had a glimpse into why it is so important to have transformative prayer—to truly work on our hearts. Prayer is an inward-outward experience. We go into ourselves to reach outward to others.

Perhaps God has hardwired us to be giving. Perhaps, when I discover my deeper self, it is my giving self.

Finding my prayer brought me to acts of kindness I had previously resisted or had never considered. Finding my prayer brought me out of myself.

There is an easy test for becoming a more spiritual human being. Are you becoming a kinder person? Do you feel the brokenness of others?

I pray for the strength to soften my heart.
I pray for the wisdom and will and love to listen
  to the prayer God is praying for me.

I pray with all of my heart for God to open
  my heart.

Who has the most open heart? Who is the most loving person you know?

We asked that question at our dining room table one Friday night, many years ago. There were eight of us: my wife, our six kids, and me, ages ranging from eight to forty-eight.

"Who is the most loving person you know?"

At once we all thought of the same person: my wife's father.

Raised in a Jewish orphanage in New Orleans, he is only capable of goodness. He gets up early to collect the neighbors' newspaper and place it on their doorstep. He listens with kindness and insight. He brings out the best in all around him.

How does someone become a loving person? How does a loving person become more loving?

The prayerful person should be the loving person. Undoing the hardness of our hearts is the work of prayer.

GUIDING QUESTIONS
FOR SELF-REFLECTION

Prayer is the "work of the heart" (Babylonian Talmud, Ta'anit 2a).

When does prayer feel like work for you?

How has your prayer life changed you?

How can I soften my heart?
How can I let others in?
How can I let God in?

When has your prayer life evoked your better self?

On a scale of 1 to 10, what number would you give to yourself regarding how hard or soft your heart is?

How does life harden your heart? How do you deal with that?

I pray for the strength to soften my heart.
I pray for the wisdom and will and love to listen to
the prayer God is praying for me.

I pray with all of my heart for God to open my heart.

Who is the most loving person you know?

How do you think they became that way?

What advice would you give to yourself to open your heart? To become more loving?

8

WHAT GETS ME STUCK?

My father is dead.

I've said Kaddish. I've sat shiva. I've passed sheloshim.
I'm getting back to normal.

No. There is no recovery from death.

"Yitgadal v'Yitkadash"
God will be great; God will be holy.

Maybe there will be a time when God will be great and
*   holy again.*
But not now. God has stopped. Death has touched me.

"Yitgadal v'Yitkadash"

Don't think I am praising God.
I AM NOT TALKING ABOUT GOD.

My Kaddish is a scream: "Look at me. I am not okay.
I am lost, shattered, shivering.
I am tamei.[6]
Do not think I have recovered. My father is dead.
I will never recover.
There will never be normal. Do you hear me?"

1945.
Death surrounds us.

There is no recovery. We cannot hear. We refuse to listen.
Death has touched us. Our Father in heaven has died.

There are not enough red heifers in the world to purify us.
We are all tamei.

For my father, I sit seven days.

For our Father in heaven, we sit seventy years.

We wait. We wait for the generations to die.

Sometimes only death can purify death.

1945–2015. Seventy years. We are getting up now.

THEMES

Accepting moments when it is hard to be prayerful

Difficult personal times

Difficult national times

Getting beyond the difficult moments

Maybe there will be a time when God will be great and holy again.
But not now. God has stopped. Death has touched me.

Today there will be no prayer. Death has stolen my soul. Mouth opens. Vocal cords don't move. No vibration. No sound.
God, I can't hear you now. I can't hear anything now.
God and I have left each other.
I don't want to be alone.
This night will have to pass by itself. Nothing can hurry it.
Time controls me.

Sometimes I get spiritually stuck. Where should I go then? Where does someone go to get spiritually unstuck?

Is there a support group for the spiritually stuck? Where is it? Am I the only one who needs it?

People throw their clichés at me:

"God never gives you a test you can't pass."

"Everything is for the best."

"You'll be stronger for this."

They are not hearing me. They don't see me. I don't need their advice. My being stuck is frightening for them. They fear my disease is contagious. I must be cured instantly.

I want someone to hear me. Someone who is not afraid to see me. I want someone to share my loneliness. I don't need words or solutions. I want someone who sees me. We could just sit together.

And most of all, I don't want to fake it. I don't want to pretend I'm present with God when I am not. I don't want just to fit in.

We pay a very great price for faking it, for saying the words without being the words. If I can fake it with God, my most intimate relationship, then who can I not fake it with?

Sometimes life gets me stuck. And there are days when I get myself stuck. Sometimes I need to be stuck. It is who I am.

On those days, I don't care about my prayer. I just want to live and eat and play and sometimes do nothing. To flake out. On those days, prayer annoys me.

Some days, others will have to shoulder the world. I'm taking a break.

Some days, it's not for me. Some days, I'm too empty, others will need to carry me. Some days, I'm too happy. I want to savor the moment. Maybe my prayer wants some days off too.

Some days I'm okay just to be. Those are my hardest days.

The sixteenth-century mystic Mirabai says, "The heat of midnight tears will bring you to God."[7]

Some nights my tears are cold. Stone cold.

1945.

Death surrounds us.

*There is no recovery. We cannot hear. We refuse
  to listen.*

*Death has touched us. Our Father in heaven
  has died.*

*There are not enough red heifers in the world to
  purify us. We are all* tamei.

The Jewish people never formally mourned for the Holocaust.
We never sat on the ground and cried and talked about the six
million. There was no time to sit *shiva.*

Maybe we were too busy building a nation. Maybe the
thought of confronting such losses was too daunting. Maybe
we had had enough of death and didn't want to dwell there
anymore.

Maybe we just didn't know what to do.

For our Father in heaven, we sit seventy years.

We wait. We wait for the generations to die.

Sometimes only death can purify death.

*1945–2015. Seventy years. We are getting
  up now.*

Can a nation get stuck? Can a nation lose its prayer?

For two thousand years, the Jewish people did not hear its prayer. We were too busy trying to survive.

What happens to a prayer deferred? Does it fade away, like a voice unheard? Or does it keep praying?

Once, in the army, my team's jeep got lost at night. They told us to shine our giant flashlight toward the sky. The rescue team saw the ray of light and found us.

Our prayer has been wandering lost for two thousand years. It is shining its light now.

Is it possible for a lost prayer to be found?

How does a nation get unstuck?

GUIDING QUESTIONS
FOR SELF-REFLECTION

My father is dead.

I've said Kaddish. I've sat shiva. I've passed sheloshim.
I'm getting back to normal.

When have you encountered obstacles in your prayer life?

What gets you stuck in prayer?

Maybe there will be a time when God will be great
and holy again.
But not now. God has stopped. Death has touched me.

When have you felt distant from God?

1945.

Death surrounds us.

*There is no recovery. We cannot hear. We refuse
to listen.*

Death has touched us. Our Father in heaven has died.

*There are not enough red heifers in the world to
purify us. We are all* tamei.

**When have you felt unworthy to pray? To be in
relationship with God?**

For my father, I sit seven days.

For our Father in heaven, we sit seventy years.

We wait. We wait for the generations to die.

Sometimes only death can purify death.

1945–2015. Seventy years. We are getting up now.

**How have tragedies of the Jewish people affected your
relationship with God? Your prayer life?**

What has helped you "get up"?

9

WHAT ABOUT THE JEWISH PEOPLE?

For two thousand years we said the silent standing prayer.
All we could hope for was to be quiet and remain standing.

We had no words.
We didn't move.

Our prayer was mute, motionless.
A petrified prayer.

Every time and place has its own soul.
Every time and place has its own prayer.

What is the soul and prayer of the Jewish people today?

Today's prayer is not silent. It is not unmoving.

Today's prayer is a loud, screaming, whistling,
    laughing prayer.
Today's prayer is a running, climbing, huffing, sweating,
    daring, risking prayer.

A moveless people needs a moveless prayer.
A moving people needs a moving prayer.

Sometimes, we lose our prayers.
Sometimes, to find our prayers, we need to lose our
    prayers again.

We have stood silently for centuries.
Not taking a step.

For the baby, the first step is the hardest.

Psychologists say the first step a baby takes is away from
its mother.
A step toward the new and unknown.

I wonder if the baby is afraid.

I know we are.

THEMES

National prayer

Waking up to the prayer of today

Changes in the Jewish people

Fear of change

For two thousand years we said the silent
standing prayer.
All we could hope for was to be quiet and
remain standing.

We had no words.
We didn't move.

Rav Abraham Isaac Kook writes that during the last many centuries, exile and persecutions battered the Jewish people, breeding excessive fear.

> Excessive fear takes away the spark of life of a
> person and all living beings. Nothing in this
> world is as bad and cruel as excessive fear . . . it is
> the source of all weakness—moral, intellectual,
> and spiritual—and paralyzes a person."[8]

Excessive fear exaggerates evil and dims beauty. It makes destruction seem present or imminent, even when it is not.

Extreme and unwarranted fear is only healed by the opposite extreme—excessive daring and chutzpah. Only by going to the opposite edge is it possible to eventually find a healthy balance of fear and courage. The excessive chutzpah in this generation may be annoying and at times infuriating, but it is needed to return the Jewish people to a state of spiritual health.

The first sign of the Messiah, writes Rav Kook, will be our witnessing the excessive chutzpah of the Jewish people.

What is the soul and prayer of the Jewish people today?

This generation has a hard time praying. I envy them.

They have seen us praying. They have seen words on the page that stay on the page. They have seen rituals of standing, bowing, chanting, and even singing, all falling empty. They have seen ceremonies of disconnection; movements without vibration.

This generation is not a generation of followers or continuers. This is not an obedient generation. This is a generation of new and now. A start-up generation.

Just because generations said it before does not make it meaningful or personal now. It does not make it mine.

This generation is shouting, "What is my prayer? Where is my prayer?" Sometimes their scream is as quiet as the rolling of eyes or the shrugging of shoulders.

We have forgotten that prayer does not begin with the words of the prayer book. Prayer does not begin with someone else's words. Prayer begins within the crevices of a yearning and broken heart. And each heart breaks differently.

This generation howls, "Should I take your medicine because it worked for you? But I have different needs. I have a different suffering."

Only God knows the pain of my heart. Only God can send me the healing and prayer I need. I need to listen and feel the sorrow and torture of my own broken heart.

Some may say this is narcissistic. Some may say this is childish and selfish. Some may say this is heretical and will be the end of Judaism. "What would happen if everyone went searching for their own prayer?!"

They say, "The Jewish people had a prayer for two thousand years. Don't be the broken link in the chain. Continue. Obey."

We continued. We obeyed. We didn't break the chain. When we were in danger, when we were in fear, when we were shamed, when we were alone, we heard our prayer. We didn't break the chain.

We bled our prayer.

We heard it so well that we still continue to hear it today, even though it is no longer the prayer God is sending to us.

We need to hear a new prayer. A prayer of voice and movement. A prayer of change, of risk. The time has come to add a new link to the chain. "Sing to God a new song" (Psalm 33:3). This is a bold and courageous generation. This generation is not fearful. God does not want us to be merely obedient.

This generation warns: "Don't give me your prayer or the prayer of your fathers. Don't give me ready-made prayer or hand-me-down prayers. Listen to me—help me find my own prayer."

This a young generation, bored of the prayers of old men. "Don't give me bearded words. Give me a young prayer. Don't give me wrinkled shriveled prayers on pale fading pages, smelling of powerless Jews running for their lives. Don't give me a petrified prayer."

We need to listen to this new generation. Our prayer begins when we finally notice: Something is not working. We have lost the way. Maybe this generation will help us find our prayer, a new prayer. Maybe they will bring the Messiah. We didn't.

What if we are so busy hearing yesterday's prayer we miss the prayer of today?

What is the soul and prayer of the Jewish people today?

Where do prayers come from?

All prayers come from Jerusalem. Jerusalem is always praying to us.

Where does your prayer go?

To Jerusalem.[9]

Wherever we are, whatever we are doing, we turn to Jerusalem. For two thousand years, wherever they were, Jews faced Jerusalem. If prayer is the "work of the heart," then the prayer of Jerusalem is the prayer of our collective heart. The heart of the Jewish people.

Prayer is all about direction. The primary prayer teaching is to direct one's heart to the Holy of Holies in Jerusalem. We direct our individual hearts to the national heart of the Jewish people.

We face Jerusalem. We open ourselves to Jerusalem. We do not pray for Jerusalem. We do not pray to Jerusalem. We let Jerusalem send us her prayers.

Jerusalem's prayer: "Look at me. Come to me. Be with me. Hope with me. Pray with me." Jerusalem sends a hope much bigger than all of the individual hopes of our lives. She sends a hope for all people. A national heart for an international hope.

My prayer: "I am opening my heart to you."

Years ago, I attended a spiritual retreat during which we were offered afternoon prayer time. We went outside and chose spots for reflection. Some people faced the forest, some the lake, some the sunset. Everyone found a place and position that worked for them. No one thought of facing Jerusalem. What prayer were they listening to?

Today's prayer is a huffing, sweating, whistling, screaming, laughing prayer.
Today's prayer is a running, climbing, swimming, daring, risking prayer.

A moveless people need a moveless prayer.
A moving people need a moving prayer.

The first prayer of the first Jew was a national prayer. A prayer of movement. A prayer of risk.

God spoke to Abraham, saying, "Leave your country, your community, and your home, and go to the land I will show you; and I will make you into a great nation" (Genesis 12:1–3).

The Torah tells us that God spoke to Abraham. I wonder how Abraham knew it was the voice of God. Was it a booming, thunderous voice? Or did the words reach Abraham through the quiet inner voice of his soul? How did Abraham know that it was God talking?

Maybe Abraham heard the very first national prayer of the Jewish people.

Maybe God is still praying a prayer of journey, risk, daring, and greatness for us?

GUIDING QUESTIONS
FOR SELF-REFLECTION

What is the soul and prayer of the Jewish people today?

How would you answer this question?

How does your relationship with the Jewish people affect your relationship with God?

Your prayer life?

Today's prayer is not silent. It is not unmoving.

Today's prayer is a loud, screaming, whistling, laughing prayer.
Today's prayer is a running, climbing, huffing, sweating, daring, risking prayer.

A moveless people need a moveless prayer.
A moving people need a moving prayer.

Would you say your soul, your prayer life, is moveless or moving? Silent or loud?

What moment or place evokes within you a moving prayer?

For the baby, the first step is the hardest.

*Psychologists say the first step a baby takes is away
from its mother.*
A step toward the new and unknown.

I wonder if the baby is afraid.

I know we are.

What new step are you afraid of?

What new step could you take in your prayer life?

10

DANCING WITH GOD

God, will you dance with me?

THEMES

Spontaneous, outrageous prayer

Getting-out-of-my-head prayer

Spiritual intimacy

That might be the most ridiculous, inane, and absurd thought that has ever crossed my mind. I'm embarrassed to look at it now.

Can I take it back? Can I unthink it? Why did I say it?

I'm looking at that line again and beginning to unravel what spontaneously burst out of me.

I want more than an intellectual relationship with God. I want more than an emotional relationship with God. I want a full experience.

I want an experience of the past, present, and future; of me and us and all of us. I want to be part of the collective dance.

And I want my private dance too.

Sometimes I wonder if I am religious or spiritual.

My religious voice talks of the big picture: family, community, and nation. Of the past and the future, of tradition and hope. My spiritual voice is very intimate. It is personal, private, and brutally honest. It focuses on the present, a string of individual moments.

When my religious life does not hear my spiritual voice, it seems as if it is just being dutiful. When my spiritual life is not working with my religious side, it seems as if I'm just following myself.

It is really hard, most of the time, to hear both of these

voices, to invite them to listen to each other. Most often they seem to be quibbling, negating, and even insulting each other.

Can these two voices live together? Sing together? Is there a dance for that?

God, that's the dance I want.

God, will you dance with me?

The poet Hafiz says:

> God and I have become like two giant fat people living in a tiny boat.
>
> We keep bumping into each other and laughing.

I want to turn the bumping and laughing into a dance. A never-ending dance.

What kind of dance would it be? Not ballet, waltz, or foxtrot. Not a dance where I'd need to remember the steps and think a lot. I don't want to overthink our dance.

What kind of music would play? Maybe *shir hashirim*—poetic, flowing, touching but not touching. Melodic. Swift. Or maybe Beethoven—movements that crescendo, gentle violins and crashing cymbals.

My family has always said I am a terrible dancer. Clumsy. Offbeat.

God, could you handle that?

How do I learn to dance with God? Is there a studio for this? Who can teach me?

Or do I need to learn by myself?

Dancing with God means not dancing alone. Responding to the presence of an "other." Always looking and listening for that mysterious "other."

Sometimes leading, sometimes following. Sometimes stepping on each other's toes.

Every life is set to its own music.

Prayer is hearing the music of my life.

A prayerful life is dancing with God.

GUIDING QUESTIONS
FOR SELF-REFLECTION

God, will you dance with me?

How would you complete this question: "God, will you
_____ _____ me?"

If you were to describe your prayer life as a state or
activity, what would you say?

When was the last time you felt like you had a "full"
relationship with God?

What does a "full" relationship with God mean to you?

God, will you dance with me?

Would you consider yourself more spiritual or more
religious?

What appeals to you in the world of spirituality?

What appeals to you in the world of religion?

When have you experienced these two voices competing
or conflicting with each other?

What could you do to find greater harmony between
spirituality and religion?

God, will you dance with me?

What does this line bring up for you: "Sometimes leading, sometimes following. Sometimes stepping on each other's toes"?

How do you think one learns to dance with God?

IV

CLOSING THOUGHTS

Writing this book changed me. It brought me to a better place. After reflecting, questioning, and writing, I have a lot more clarity. It's clear to me what was missing; what had brought me to a place of losing my prayer.

I realized that I was praying a prayer, but not my prayer. I was afraid to fully embrace my inner voice.

I lost my prayer because I had lost myself. I did not trust myself. I didn't trust the soul that God had given me. I had become a stranger to my own soul; I wasn't listening to the voice of my own inner wisdom.

I had been listening so well to the voice of the tradition and the voice of God that I needed to escape. Sometimes we need to run away in order to find ourselves.

I realized that sometimes I listen too much to the external voice and lose myself; but sometimes I listen too much to my own inner voice and find myself running for too long from God. To find my prayer, I sought not to abandon the wisdom of centuries, nor to listen exclusively to my own needs and desires. I needed to find balance.

I sought soulful well-being in the form of harmony between the two voices: the outer wisdom of centuries of tradition with the inner wisdom of my soul, the *Tzelem Elokim* that the Creator of the world has gifted me.

The process of writing this book has restored my inner life. It's been slow, with a lot of pausing, writing, and being open to confronting my most frightening inner truths.

But I am beginning to hear the music of both voices again, feeling proud and rewarded for not running away. It is easier to ditch something when it is not working or has seemingly outlived its usefulness.

Sometimes the lost prayers bring us to the prayers of the found.

My prayer now is that some of these harmonic vibrations reach you, wherever your body and soul may be.

APPENDIX I

THE TWO STAGES OF
JEWISH SPIRITUALITY TODAY

There are two stages in the development of a full spiritual life. During the last several generations, the Jewish world has become very adept at the first stage of Jewish spirituality—the stage of connection. The time has now come to move to the second—the stage of calling.

This book of reflections aims at moving the spiritual conversation from stage 1 to stage 2: from connection to calling.

We want spiritual connection. We want to be connected to something beyond ourselves.

When I ask people for their first association with the word *spirituality*, the most common response is *"Connection."* They speak of connecting to something beyond themselves, whether with nature, history, a people, a transcendent being, or even the depth and fullness of the present moment. We live in an awesome and inspiring world.

The experience of spiritual connection is presently dominating the Jewish community and language today. Many practices currently exist that can help bring an individual to spiritual connection, including journaling, meditation, and daily mindfulness routines. Spending reflective time in nature and yoga are also valuable and effective tools for deepening spiritual connection.

Connection can bring about a deeper state of calm, serenity, and fullness. In Abraham Joshua Heschel's words, spiritual connection can lead to a life of wonder and radical amazement. Spiritual connection can also be personally rewarding, leading to a sense of greater self-worth, gratitude, love, and compassion, though the shadow sides of spiritual connection—self-absorption and narcissism—can take hold as well.

Spiritual connection begins with pausing and noticing.

Our spiritual role models in the Torah paused and noticed. According to the Midrash (Rabbah 39), Abraham's generation did not see what he saw. He stopped and observed how the world functioned. Moses, too, was the only person to pause and behold the burning bush, even though it was visible to all who passed by (Exodus 3).

Abraham and Moses *noticed*, and they followed up by asking themselves questions. Abraham asked, "Could this mansion be glowing and not have an owner?" Moses asked, "Why isn't this bush burning up?" Abraham and Moses noticed, stopped, reflected, and then articulated their astonishment. This led to their *personal connection* with God.

But this connection was *not* the end goal. God caught their attention *in order to communicate with them*:

> "God called to Abraham and said: 'I am the owner of the palace.'"

"God saw that Moses turned to see, and God called to him from within the bush and said, 'Moses, Moses!'"

After stopping, noticing, and articulating their amazement, both Abraham and Moses were then called to mission by God—they were called to action and purpose.

God said to Abraham, "*Lech-lecha* (leave your home) … and through you all the families of the world will be blessed" (Genesis 12:1). God tells Moses to return to Egypt and save his brethren (Exodus 3).

Personal connection led to hearing the call, which led to active living and purpose. The first stage of the spirituality of connection is meant to culminate in the second stage, the spirituality of calling.

What is the spirituality of calling?

God has sent each of us into this world for a purpose (or *tikkun*, "healing"), which only our unique personality can fulfill. The world is a work in progress, and we have a role in its repairing. God has implanted within each of us a unique soul that is continually communicating—calling us, guiding and directing how we should act. Through the voice of our soul we are guided to become who we were destined to be; to play our unique role in healing this world. Calling leads to purpose, mission, and a life of action.

If today's emphasis on the spirituality of connection is about entering the *fullness of the world*, then the spirituality of calling wants to bring us into becoming fully present in the *brokenness* of the world.

The experience of *calling* is fundamentally different from the experience of *connection*:

- Connection speaks to our private inner self; calling speaks to our public responsibility and leads to action.

- Connection begins when the individual stops and notices; calling begins with God's reaching out.

- Connection is a response to the beauty and wonder of the world; calling is a response to the missing and needed in the world.

- Connection engenders feelings of tranquility, fullness, and gratitude; calling engenders feelings of fear, anxiety, and doubt that we may not be worthy of or cannot fulfill the calling.

- Connection brings one to a state of being; calling brings one to a state of action.

- Connection brings one into the immediate present; calling brings one to the future.

- Connection brings one to dwell in the moment; calling brings one to journey

How do we hear this call?

We are not prophets. We can never be fully certain that what we hear or sense is the true voice of our soul, or that we are really hearing what God wants us to do. Yet every now and then, there are moments of intuitive clarity. Rav Abraham Isaac Kook writes that this voice is continually whispering to us, singing to us, and praying for us. As long as we are alive, our soul is always calling to us.

Unfortunately, there are serious obstacles that often prevent us from hearing this voice, from sensing the calling. Perhaps the biggest obstacle is our reluctance to talk personally about our relationship with God.

I think the most essential role of educators today is to remove this obstacle that inhibits us; to create spaces in which people feel more comfortable talking about their relationship with God. We need to invite people to share how God plays a role in their lives.

Rabbis and educators, our own spiritual-calling moments must be the root of this conversation. We need to share with our students when we have been open to hearing our inner voices. As risky as it feels, as educators we must engage students on our personal *lech-lechas*. We must model being on the journey, open to risk taking and uncertainty, willing to listen to the voices of our souls and daring to walk with, and before, God.

We want stage 1; we want spiritual connection. God created an awesome and inspiring world to behold. Becoming fully present in each moment is essential to living a spiritual life. And going inward, into ourselves, is really ultimately about going outward, in service of others. The state of *being* is the prelude to the state of *action*. If the spiritual connection does not lead to action benefiting others, it becomes self-serving.

Connection-only spirituality can become intoxicating, self-absorbed, and narcissistic. The time has come to move the conversation of spirituality from connection to calling, from self to others, from *being* to *acting*. Our spirituality needs to propel us into the brokenness of the moment; to accept the world's invitation for us to step in.

APPENDIX II

EDUCATING TOWARD
A PRAYERFUL LIFE

If I were to teach children how to lead a prayerful life, I wouldn't begin with the synagogue service. I'd begin with the natural world.

I'd take them outside. I'd invite them to walk and look at the world with eyes of wonder. I'd ask them to find things that catch their eye; things that make them say "Wow"— what I call "the fingerprints of God." Things that carry a sense of mystery; things that invite us to look deeper, beyond what we know.

I'd invite the kids to pause, notice, and reflect.

After they found their "wonder objects," I'd invite them to sit and contemplate. To choose one and think about its history, its daily life, its future. I'd invite them to imagine the object speaking. To listen deeply and use their imagination. What is it saying? What is its message to them?

I'd invite them to write about it. And then share what they wrote with a friend.

If I were to teach children how to pray with *kavana* (intention), I wouldn't begin with the prayer book. I would begin with their own words of prayer.

I'd ask them to write a short poem to God. And then a short poem from God to them. For those who find it difficult to write, I'd invite them to draw their poem or sculpt it from clay.

Imagine if kids formed a habit of reflecting on their inner lives, listening to what comes up and then expressing those thoughts, without fear of criticism or judgment.

When children engage in a creative journey without knowing exactly where it will lead, they are actually setting out on a journey of faith just like that of Abraham, to whom God said, "Go ... to the land that I will show you."

If I were to teach someone how to have a relationship with God, I wouldn't begin with the Torah. I would begin with their own experience.

I would take them to the desert. To sit and listen to the silence. To feel the wind. To breathe the simplicity. To enter into the eternal timelessness. To be with the source of being. To return to where it all began.

Most important, if I were to teach children how to lead a prayerful life, pray with *kavana*, and have a relationship with God, I wouldn't begin with the kids. I'd begin by learning, struggling, and discovering all of these things—for myself.

Acknowledgments

These reflections emerged from a *chevruta* with my daughter, Lilach, studying Rav Kook's approach to prayer. Thank you, Lilach, for creating the space for your Abba to explore his inner life.

Thank you to all my children and their beloveds —Shachar and Zev, Ma'ayan and Elishav, Amichai and Melody, Yaniv and Adi, Ra'aya and Noam, and Lilach—who do not waver when their father tumbles through his spiritual worlds.

The Ayeka team—Yehoshua, Dasee, Shira, Leora, and Ilana—supported this project, offered unconditional love, and precious wisdom.

Emily Wichland, you professionally and graciously brought this manuscript to its final form. You made every correction a pleasure to witness.

Jen Klor and Daphna Awadish, you are the dynamic duo of graphics and illustration. You transformed the words into visual beauty.

To Roger Housden, thank you for offering the inspiration behind these ten reflections and broader reflections. Your books are a daily lesson in honesty and authenticity.

I am indebted to all those who have worked, struggled, and sacrificed to create a vibrant home for the Jewish people that allows me the freedom to experiment and explore my inner worlds without the fear of jeopardizing the future of Judaism.

And finally, my faithful traveler, Sara Yehudit. This book expresses the words and work of my heart. I did not have a heart till I met you, so many cycles of life ago. *Mwah.*

Notes

1. Abraham Isaac Kook, *Lights of Holiness*, vol. 2 (Jerusalem: Mossad HaRav Kook, 1984), 230, 235.

2. A reference to the James Joyce character Mr. Duffy in *Dubliners* (Smyrna, DE: Prestwick House, 2006). The original: "Mr. Duffy lived a short distance from his body."

3. Mary Oliver, "Have You Ever Tried to Enter the Long Black Branches?" in *West Wind: Poems and Prose Poems* (New York: Mariner Books, 1998).

4. Avraham Kook, *Mo'adei HaRa'ayah: Writings of Rav Avraham Kook*, ed. Rav Moshe Zvi Neria (B'nei Barak: Tzela, 1991), 237.

5. Babylonian Talmud, Ta'anit 2a.

6. Leviticus 21.

7. Mirabai, "The Heat of Midnight Tears," translated by Robert Bly.

8. Avraham Kook, *Ikvei Hatzon* (Jerusalem: Mossad HaRav, 1985), 119.

9. Mishnah, Brachot 4:5, 6.

The *Ayeka* Story

Aryeh Ben David was born in the United States and moved to Israel in 1978. He received rabbinical ordination from the Israeli Rabbinate. He was senior staff and director of spiritual education at the Pardes Institute in Jerusalem from 1987 to 2003. From 2003 to 2006 he served as the rabbinical educational consultant for Hillel International. He is the author of *Around the Shabbat Table: A Guide to Fulfilling and Meaningful Shabbat Table Conversations, The Godfile: 10 Approaches to Personalizing Prayer, Becoming a Soulful Educator,* and *Hearing Your Own Voice: The Ayeka Haggadah.*

In 2008, he founded *Ayeka*: Center for Soulful Education. Ayeka enables individuals, educators, and parents to combine Jewish wisdom with inner life wisdom to hear the authentic voice of their soul.

Ayeka's mission is to provide the tools to breathe life into Jewish text study and enable a personally relevant, meaningful, and life-impacting experience. To do this, we need to recognize that the mind learns differently than the heart, effective learning also engages our souls, and the ultimate goal of acquiring Jewish knowledge is to impact our everyday lives.

Ayeka provides the opportunity for Jews of all backgrounds and affiliations to engage in a reflective study of Torah and Jewish wisdom, to discover their daily purpose and life calling, and to take measured steps to become their more authentic aspirational selves through this process. We are all works-in-progress, and Jewish wisdom is the key to our becoming our better selves.

Ayeka ("Where are you?) was created to provide this opportunity. *Ayeka's* program tracks include:

- Becoming a Soulful Individual

- Becoming a Soulful Family

- Becoming a Soulful Educator

Participants include rabbis, educators, Jewish professionals, parents, grandparents, and individual learners from every denomination who want more; they are seeking a method of engaging with traditional Jewish wisdom that enables them to clarify their own unique paths and purpose, one that impacts and enhances their lives.